The Cellist, a Bellydancer
& Other Distractions

Also by Libby Sommer and published by Ginninderra Press
My Year With Sammy (2015)
The Crystal Ballroom (2017)
The Usual Story (2018)
Stories From Bondi (2019)
Lost In Cooper Park (2020)

Libby Sommer

The Cellist, a Bellydancer & Other Distractions

For Les Murray
in memory

With gratitude to poet Norm Neill
for his insights and gentle guidance

The Cellist, a Bellydancer & Other Distractions
ISBN 978 1 76109 325 8
Copyright © text Libby Sommer 2022
Cover image: Gerhard Lipold

First published 2022 by
Ginninderra Press
PO Box 3461 Port Adelaide 5015
www.ginninderrapress.com.au

Contents

Foreword	9
The Cellist	11
His Coriander	12
Quarantine	13
Survival	14
Someone I Don't Know Sideswiped My Car	15
Amber Puppy	16
Taste	18
Sixteen Is a Very Difficult Age, You Know	19
Between the Islands of the Pacific	20
Elsewhere	21
Lying On a Harbour Beach At Noon	22
Renewal	23
The Ladder and Its Dangers	24
In the Mall	25
Her Amber Necklace	26
Bronte Beach	27
The Neighbours	29
On the Last Day of 2020	31
Last Summer	32
White Ibis	34
That's all you can do	35
Words of Love	37
Restless	38
Trajectory	39
Inheritance	40
Not Long Now	42
Because of Councils We Can Ask For Things	43
Weekend Escape	44

Because of Imagination	45
My Neighbour's Special Coffee Shop	46
While Flattening the Curve	48
The Road Back	50
Waiting	51
Here	52
Do You Want To Try Me Out?	53
Safe… The Pandemic	54
Morning Storm	55
The Bellydancer	56
Change	58
End	60
This is what it feels like	61
Taking a Chance	62
My Friend Is Swiping & Scrolling	63
Distraction	65
Hostilities	66
Acknowledgements	67
About the Author	69

If you aren't in over your head,
how do you know how tall you are?
– T.S. Eliot

Foreword

Many years ago, as part of a Masters in Writing, I enrolled in a poetry class. Plunging into poetry changed both me and my writing.

The forty-five poems in *The Cellist, a Bellydancer & Other Distractions* celebrate the beauty and diversity of urban Australian contemporary life – its twists and turns, distractions and disturbances. The poems explore the quirks of human behaviour in love and in oneness with nature.

The Cellist

I was grudgingly ancient. Not older, wiser and ancient. But easily recognisable as ancient. Skin was the culprit – the human body's largest organ. I had his mobile number and he had mine, the cellist from the seniors' dating site. I examined its configuration. Was there a pattern I needed to decode? I hated initiating, but he needed reassurance. It might take him forever to ring. Composing a text, my palms sweated. My heart thumped. Was he okay with texting? I hated my impatience. I hated my unexpected fragility. I sent the text. Yesterday's meet-up was fun. I'd like to go for a ride on your motorbike sometime, although the helmet will squash my hair.

Then I worried I'd gone too far. My legs wrapped around him on a bike? I sounded like a whore. A desperado. A woman too long without a man. His reply was immediate. Had he been holding the phone in his hand? We can start with a short ride around the block. I've got a large helmet. Everyone gets hat hair.

I don't want you to go on his motorbike, my daughter warned. I'll go for a ride on his bike, my granddaughter offered. What sort of boat's he got? A tinnie or a sail boat? asked my grandson. I googled 'what to expect when riding pillion'. Hang on. Brace for braking and acceleration by holding on to the rider's waist. Bikes must lean to corner. Relax. Tyres provide plenty of grip.

We had dinner, exchanged silly jokes, leaned towards each other, went back to my place – and had incredible sex. The sensitivity of a stringed instrumentalist was really something else. If I knew how, I would have burst into song.

His Coriander

Flourishing above the planter box, it's ready for harvesting.
I snip the curling tendrils with their skinny stalks,
hearing the clean snap of stem from dense green foliage.
At the end of a rain-filled night, the earth smells heady.
He took his suitcase, his cello, and his sheet music.
He left the fragrant coriander seeds,
said, Tending a relationship is like keeping a plant alive.
So I'll take this herb
inside to the kitchen and chop it.
I'll disperse it piece by piece with my hands,
the longed-for exotic spice of citrus and curry.
I'll be forever grateful for escape
from my infatuation
with coriander.

Quarantine

But there still are the other things –
water's rhythmic tumble
over rocks,
the gentle hush of wind through leaves –
we celebrate
in solitude.

Survival

More gusts of wind
through new high-rises
sharp-edged.

More traffic,
more construction dust
much overshadowing
in grey & black.

Newly planted in the local streets
the bottlebrush should know why it exists:
nectar feeding of insects,
of butterflies & birds.

East of the city
blue beaches dazzle & swell.
They re-emerge
in a spring break-out

giving hope to the lone crimson flower
squeezing through densely-packed leaves.

Someone I Don't Know Sideswiped My Car

Bad luck recently, you could say, after surviving some extremely unfortunate luck. For hours I sat across from you in the Emergency Bay: your face dripping with blood. They gave you a compress to stop the flow of red from your cheekbones and your nose. Every time you touched your face, it opened up the wound. Punched in both eyes and the nose. A robbery as you walked home, I hear you tell your girlfriend on the mobile. And then you're telling the emergency nurse you can't wait any longer to see a doctor. 'You may have concussion,' she cautioned.

Did you find your way home?

For days I wonder how you are. I sniff the first spring jasmine hanging over the fence and your girlfriend whom I've never met crowds my thoughts, till one day, peering out my bedroom window, I notice someone has sideswiped my car. Not exactly what I'd expected to see but, man, the wisteria are showing their purple blooms. A nervous possum balances on the telephone line above the road and there's a newspaper article about an elderly cyclist who died after a freak bike accident caused by a swooping magpie.

Bad luck that a second vehicle crashed into my car while it waited at the smash repair place. Look up, take care, someone or something you don't know may sideswipe you or punch you in the nose.

Amber Puppy

What can an amber puppy mean in a world of Siris and driverless cars?

I was older, one of the Baby Boomers. Life was a series of warnings: Don't fall over rugs or loose cords, don't overeat, don't go to bed before nine, drink coffee after midday, watch too much Netflix. When the new puppy arrived one birthday, rich brown as a raisin, I heard it shadowing me: Don't trip on the dog's lead.

There was much to be anxious about. One day, walking through the park – the rain had eased, spring waterfalls spilled into the creek, soon we would cool off under the trees – I lost my grip on the lead. Into the bushes he fled, disappearing into green. Since when did parks swallow small dogs? I drove home in a frantic car. My best friend. I'd loved him and he'd loved me.

The days staggered past like drunks. I prayed silently, absorbed sunshine, climbed steps, wrote Letters to the Editor. Don't panic, don't shallow breathe, don't think the worst – you could hear it all around. A reclining Buddha could show you how to deepen the breath. A bird call at first light could tell you when to get up. A storm could remember to fill the dams and the water tanks – I was meandering between the trees when I saw him scampering through the creek. Splashing around then shaking himself dry. A muddy escapee. A barking survivor.

Where had he been these three long days? I could wash him, wrap him in a towel, take him home. Unexpected good news could still happen. Dogs off-the-leash need to stay close to their mistresses. Trees shed their leaves in winter and dogs run away, but find their way back. Seventy-two hours later, what can an amber puppy tell you in a world of Botox and identity theft?

See the difference between holding on and losing your grip.

Taste

I rather like poems about minor calamities, bursts of tiny delights, the sun warming the tender skin of the elderly. Also, the way palm fronds conduct themselves during a southerly, dishevelled, exposing the softness of their billowing arms. Pastries in display cases do something for me too. Even cupcakes iced in gelato colours, adorned with miniature decorations… Can you see my preference for the words 'miniature' and 'tiny', an inclination towards the distilled in a world favouring often the big and the overwhelming? People with the patience to follow a complex recipe – well, that's not me, but I like to taste what they cook. Babies in prams kicking chubby legs make me hover – how difficult not to take a bite. If you write something about a paper straw, I will be fascinated. You could try a ladybird, a pocket-size umbrella. The generalised angst of the human condition, however, may be hard for me to get a handle on. Watch that man with the disabled daughter moisten his finger after her cupcake is eaten and relish the last crumbs. Consider the rainbow-coloured wristband tied to a letterbox on the way to the park or the miniature plastic bucket and spade we found half-hidden on the beach at Bronte and packed with us for years on every visit to the sea.

Sixteen Is a Very Difficult Age, You Know

Well yes it is. This time of year isn't easy either. It has most of us by the neck. You don't want to get sick at Christmas. They said he needs six weeks of intensive therapy then they'll decide about medication. How – when everything's closed till February? Yes, he's up and down. Better some days, but hardly ever. They said hide all the tablets and remove the kitchen knives. I ring or text to see how he's going. He doesn't always pick up. Don't refer to the incident. Wait for him to say something. Well, he doesn't say much though he'll let me give him a hug – sometimes. So here I am trying to gather his forgotten dreams from the air. They're drifting just outside my reach.

Between the Islands of the Pacific

Because by now we know everything is not so blue
out here.

The cities had tipped rubbish into the sea,
and we let them without even noticing.

Not even feeling our breathing clear
as gusts reaching ten knots cleaned up our days.

Not even. Today pure blue sky, blue sea,
out there the horizon drawing a line
below the clouds, the absoluteness of it. Nights
of diesel engines shuddering beneath us.

We lounge on chairs side by side on the deck.
At dusk, we stand at the railing of the ship as the sun
slips into the ocean. In the fresh sea air, their backs turned,
some raise a selfie-stick or light a cigarette while others
stand holding their breath.

Where can we go from here, and how?

Elsewhere

Hair remembers how dark a room becomes
when hair is not let loose, straw fallen from the head
of a broom, drifting onto a path,
crunched underfoot by someone who never realised
it was straw. Hair drank, jogged,
ate by itself, knew how to tick 'Like'
on social media. But hair felt
out of touch with itself
unable to distinguish the difference between
fear of the unknown, and fear of something
bad. Hair remembered the ultramarine blue of sea and sky
and the hundred varieties of tuna, calamari and squid.

Hair has dreams, that's what hair does.
Covers over a shiny scalp, frames the face.
Adventure means exploration and discovery.
And hair remembers – blankets of humidity, harsh light,
residing there in the brain's temporal lobes.
Even now, when hair is back home,
it remembers the wanting things to remain the same
but gives thanks for faraway places
where you can untangle and restyle yourself.

Lying On a Harbour Beach At Noon

There is an opening out of the self which happens
when the sun is high in a cloudless blue
and its warmth sinks into the body.

It occurs on a gentle beach.
It is a slow opening,
like waking up in
your own cosy apartment.
When all the tenants wake up
and the blinds snap
the windows open wide.
If you are in bed you struggle to open to the bright light.
If you are elsewhere, feeling your separateness, alienated,
you long for home and think you're falling apart.

You are not falling apart.
You could open into your own particular self,
feel your skin move away from the bone,
your belly like an open wound tightening
then opening with everything exposed.
You know you can stop the empty grasping if you want to
because you have a deep knowing,
you open to it, and for now
it holds you gently.

Renewal

To walk
with a heavy step.
Needing nothing
a credit card can buy
but wanting to be
somewhere new.

Seeing the same old things
you've explored to death.
Imagining yourself
someplace else
breathing in
a new perspective.

A regenerated self
could see differently.
But what would that do to
the old self still following
in its own footsteps?

The Ladder and Its Dangers

It's dizzying up there. You climb to the top shelves for whatever your mood requires: on loneliness, weight reduction, a book of Basho's Haiku and find half a dozen books you forgot you had which side tracks the initial quest, since now that you've located them you have to consider them. Will I ever reread this, recycle it in the street library? Of course, your reading interests are very different from the interests you had when you placed it alphabetically on the shelf. Perhaps your interests have moved in a different direction now, maybe they've become more multicultural. Perhaps you think continuing to read Anita Brookner and her stories of loss and aloneness are not the best choice for you any more. Your quest takes on a sedentary nature as you sit on the floor to search the lower shelves, scanning titles and author names. Possibly by now you've been up and down the ladder several times and been peering upwards for extended periods cutting off the blood supply to your neck. And you've stood up too quickly from the floor and are feeling totally off balance. Now you need to consider blood sugar levels, blood pressure, PEOPLE OVER SIXTY SHOULDN'T CLIMB LADDERS. Discombobulated for a while, you're too preoccupied to recall what sent you up the ladder in the first place.

In the Mall

In a café inside a mall in Sydney a small curly-topped girl sobbed and sobbed. She sat on her father's lap, stabbing her finger into a slice of banana bread. Her dad soothed, whispered, coaxed. What would you like, Tara? He cut into his poached egg. Toast? he cajoled. The girl sobbed more loudly, wailing, coughing, staring out into the mall. I want my mum. She cuddled a pink soft piglet. Our eyes scanned the glass display of croissants, pies and pastries. I loved every carb that did not pass my lips. I loved the sobbing child who heard no one else in that café but herself, whose lungs fought hard to reach a soaring, sorrowful pitch. What have you got? an elderly woman asked her. Still crying, the child held up her toy. Her father gave up on his poached eggs and carried her out, still wailing. We went and sat at the table with the stabbed-at bread her finger had made and swept the moist crumbs into a heap.

Her Amber Necklace

my mother's dead
my mother's dead my brother said
he jumped in the air and
clicked his heels together

her children and grandchildren
and great grandchildren all came
jumping and bouncing
on forbidden chairs

we all laughed

now
distant lights scatter black night
a bus rumbles up Bondi Road
clock ticks in the empty kitchen
only the ticking
then
a dog barks outside

her woollen jumper warms me
her amber necklace hugs my neck

Bronte Beach

The surf's been hammered by rain,
and along the pavement open-faced cafés wedge side by side:
compact, glass-fronted, in flattened
Art Deco buildings, with competing blackboard menus.
Rain drips from the edge of the canvas awning,
and a smell of fried fish in rancid oil
through the mouth of the sliding door
as an oversized bus pulls in and blocks the view.

On both sides of the road,
hungry meters demand vigilance.
Cars parked, close-knit as train carriages,
in the monotones of modern home interiors.

The sun loses its way behind grey cloud,
far from the haze-filled horizon.
Marooned on the swell are wet-suited board riders,
unwavering as the cliff face
above the rocks that define the beach.
Beyond the rock pool the waves
remain stubbornly low spreading a shallow calm.
The rain settles, rusting roof racks in the salt air,
and those expired meters will upset the fattened
people-who-lunch in the darkening afternoon.

All day the treacherous ocean scours
the man-made sea pool, where
all-weather swimmers scan the water
for migrating dolphins or whales.
A white-hulled speedboat appears
in the grey-blue, travelling north,
and the black-clad board riders wait,
grounded, legless pigeons who can,
in a heartbeat, fan their iridescent wings.

Squabbling seagulls swoop and dive
and chase each other between the palms,
each white slow and steady flap of wings
picked up by the whiteness of the backwash
of the speed boat out there on the pastel-pink ocean,
disappearing behind the haze.

The Neighbours

When cicadas burrow below the rusting tennis totem
what does that say to you about a mother and a father?

The ball, bound to the totem's string,
loses its balance in the soggy grass

where a boy and his father hit
to each other around the tennis pole

as cicadas tunnel and feed beneath the earth.
Now, nobody bats the ball. Where has the father gone?

Maybe the door to the top-floor unit opens and the boy comes out.
The mother comes out wiping sweat from her face.

She's carried all the bags downstairs as there's no one else now,
to lift them. Besides the woman and the boy.

The tennis ball hangs limp in the breeze
and a kookaburra lands on the clothes line

as a small lizard darts beneath the tomato plant
and other cast-off bags and children's broken toys

are piled up
by the side of the road but there is not a boy

playing in the backyard with his father.
How will that change things around here?

If the kookaburra laughs just as you open your eyes.
If at dawn something scurries in the hallway

and frightens you and it is a cockroach
and you remember you didn't wash the dishes

then what exactly does that mean
about the sort of neighbour you've turned into?

On the Last Day of 2020

Truncated morning,
thick white mist masks the valley.
What greater luck than to walk with freedom
on mountain paths?
Passing hydrangea shrubs
lining the edge of the park –
you could sit on a rain-soaked bench.
Drinking hot chocolate beside
the acidic blue and alkaline pink bushes,
I thought we would have certainty by 2021.

What a dream to keep thinking by next autumn
by next year
before next winter
before the swallows leave the coast
My neighbour says this time last year
we wondered if we'd lose our homes in the fires.

When the mountain mist descended,
we knew the light rain would moisten
the dry summer earth and inspire new greening.
We know hydrangeas change colour
according to the state of the soil.
A white one will stay white
for its entire life, but may develop
pale pink ageing tones
just when the calendar is due to turn.

Last Summer

A woman at a wharf
with a beer in her hand

listens as waves pound
the old wooden ferry side to side.

Each makes a sharp,
slapping sound against the hull.

Have the mighty swells at beaches
been embraced by the harbour?

This woman who has received
a message from her son:

I can't call you.
I'm drowning.

has a sudden fear of the waves.
If the surf conditions are hazardous,

if the heatwave continues today and tomorrow,
some beaches unpatrolled,

if no cool change arrives from the south-west…
By then her reply to her son

may be lying unopened in his phone.
People know to swim between the red and yellow flags,

but what about those fishing or standing
on rock platforms not wearing a life jacket?

She doesn't know how deep the water is
or how fast the current is flowing.

White Ibis

We wish that nature could stay put
in their home, far away…
not urban tip turkeys, bin chickens –
not like us,
scrounging for a living in cities,
but stay where they thrive,
feeding in swamps, lagoons,
floodplains & grasslands
their black downward-curved bills
digging for crayfish and mussels.

The farmers' friend,
featherless black heads
flocking in V-shaped flight
to locust-afflicted areas,
gorging on ravaging hordes of insects.
Unlike us, they can eliminate
plagues with ease.

There are nights when we fall asleep
dreaming of ibises
flying back home.

That's all you can do

The news reports:
at watch and act today
total fire ban
smoke haze   poor air quality
asthma sufferers
and other respiratory problems
stay indoors.

Hot north westerly winds
west and south-west of Sydney
properties cleared and prepared
an anxious night   distant sirens
confusion
to leave or to go
Springwood, Yarramundi.

Residents report:
rescue our animals
and get out of here
a new fire break
it's always your family
that's more important
pack up your photos,
that's all you can do
temporary accommodation
photos are what you've seen
and experienced.

On amber watch today
200 houses destroyed so far
hoping and praying for the best
containment lines,
will they hold?

Exhausted fire fighters
people's lives are the most important
fire crews keep back-burning
what else can you do?

Despite ember attacks on homes
Rural Fire Service to link up
bushfires as winds drop.

Today has started off cool.

Words of Love

How a fierce outburst
might shock then hover
in the between spaces of
cumulus phrases, flashes
of dark clarity,
whatever is said,
try 'infatuation', or 'forgiveness',
any word you clutched
or exchanged so its underbelly
remained hidden.
So you held on tight
down a storm and it saved you
from drowning. Without this
the years would be batter
circling doughnuts afloat in boiling oil,
but without the icing.

Restless

The sun lit skyward-reaching
buildings into cloudless blue
as a white pickup truck, its load
secured by a shiny tarpaulin,
sped up when the traffic lights turned to amber.

We, at a café on the side of that road,
looked up as the morning walkers
in their backward-facing baseball caps
stood too close to the kerb waiting to cross
when the truck's brakes hissed as it
clipped the corner.

In that near-miss bright busyness
we breathed out the vehicle
exhaust fumes that would irritate our eyes
whenever the city bore down on us,
choke our lungs, or screech
it's time…pack your bags and get out of there.

Trajectory

I still find myself googling words
like 'growth'. A day's growth of unshaven
dark stubble on his chin.

A bougainvillea buds green after sentence pruning.
Speak from the heart – I'm all ears.

The paragraph cuts its flowery prose.

*

Recently, when the doctor wound a blood
pressure sleeve around my arm,
she told me I'm a genius. She thought
her words would make me smile.

Have I made your day? The thing
is, you live inside your head.

I forced my gaze out the window
to a line of trees on either side of a road
their connecting branches an archway of fettered leaves.

A pathway. That's what I need.

Inheritance

From my father I have inherited the ability
to stand at the races and watch.

Look, he says, see them round the straight.
There's the favourite. My father says he's no
gambler, but he loves adrenalin's kick.

His horse makes a break from
out wide. Wins by a nose.
That's how I live my life.
I like to stay on its fringes.

From my mother, an obsession with mental
arithmetic. We must add and subtract
and multiply in our heads.
You don't know about my mathematical abilities.
It's something I do when you're elsewhere.

The calculator rests idle in my desk drawer,
batteries deadened from lack of engagement
like someone who feels unloved.

Thanks to my mother I am quick to estimate profit
and loss. When share prices plunge, I do not
crystallise my losses. Isn't that supposed to show
a head for numbers?

My mother does the cryptics, which I just can't do.
But locating a pattern in a series
of numbers gives me a buzz. A return to
pencil, paper and eraser.

We had family discussions
about prevailing weather conditions and the track —
the weather, the jockeys, the trainers and the track
in Sydney and in Melbourne.
I've shared my winnings
ever since.

Not Long Now

'The great gift of Easter is hope.' – Basil C. Hume

I dipped one finger in the jar of indecision. On the streets of the autumn-cooled city a wheelchair-bound man pushed himself into a café. Two twenty-something sisters shepherding three small boys behave yourself or we'll go home paid compassionate attention to each other. April was just beginning. One loosened her neck scarf. She could see herself in her sister's eyes. Sunday school children ate bunny-shaped chocolates. A waitress set a wooden HAPPY EASTER sign on a table by the door, straightening her rabbit-ear headband.

Here they were again. Shelves of supermarket chocolates. Aisles and aisles. Foil-wrapped eggs and rabbits of all sizes. I felt no need to 'treat myself' to red specials. Countdown days stung us into action. What about the little people on our long list? How much junk food should we give them this year? The days say we will agonise and agonise. I dug my finger into the jar of indecision, it said don't sweat the small stuff.

Because of Councils We Can Ask For Things

Someone has been placing a draft
letter to Council on the tables at the café
by the tennis courts anchored by glass pots
of sugar cubes, complaining about
the number of boats left on the street leading to the park.

The wide boats present a traffic hazard
for cars trying to drive through the narrow street.

These boats are permanently parked there
and most are covered in cobwebs.
As constant users of the park facilities
for tennis, walking and coffee… We have
all complained to Council over an extended period
and hope you will assist us on this occasion.

Good luck to the polite letter-writer.

On the street where I live nearby the road is
made narrow when modern cars park
on both sides. We suggested speed humps
but the road remains flat as ever.

Does the letter-writer still visit the park
handing out her draft letter hoping to inspire
others, or is she waiting and wishing for a miracle?

Daily the thin sky writes
'this is the way things go'

Weekend Escape

Old bar fridges in motel rooms can ruin your holiday. The first night of a weekend alone, a scuttering sound wakes you with a start. Has someone entered the room? Your stomach tightens. You lie there paralysed under the doona. Maybe it was only a mouse. Dozing, you shout HELP! in a nightmare. There is no one to hear you scream. You've left your partner at home. You toss and turn not knowing what to do. By now fingers of dawn are parting the heavy curtains. You breathe deep into your belly. The terror releases its grip. In the morning warmth the fridge stops its humming and temperature adjustments. Turn the fridge to zero before going to bed. But the fridge will defrost and separate the yoghurt into two halves, one watery, the other like cheese curds. When the fridge is defrosting be careful you don't slip on the wet tiles in front. A towel on the floor will do the trick. You miss his wise counsel, but you know now what needs to be done.

Because of Imagination

She is clasping the books close to her chest,
carrying them home across the tiled mall,
then up the frantic hill.
If another person stares, she will hide herself
behind the books.

She'd asked the aproned librarian to find
a new mystery and a drama for her mother.
When her parents start their arguing,
on their return from work,
she will escape to her bedroom.
Her family of dolls are waiting.
Fantasies upon fantasies.

She is carrying the books past the church
and the barbecue chicken place.
What this city withholds from her
her imagination will provide: a big sister,
a library full of happy endings.
The books have already told their stories,
stories of struggle contained within their covers.

When the couches rearrange themselves
as a special place for dreaming,
and the hammering and the drilling in the street
have faded into silence,

she will not feel adrift.
She will have dreams to remember
and remember and remember.

My Neighbour's Special Coffee Shop

Thick layer of chocolate blanketing the milk froth,
what reassurance to be known in person by Hyun,
his hands gloved and his face masked,
to be known as the small cap with no lid,
without speaking.
What a joy while quarantined alone –
anything for acknowledgement by another.

My neighbour stood at a railing,
I can't stop saying – how I need this routine.
She sipped at the takeaway, licking the rim.
She should be staying put at home,
except for essential trips out. But she
was addicted to the morning coffee ritual.
I can't stop saying – I know I'm repeating myself. But
then she'd say it again.

She dressed in her activewear every single day,
to prove she was out exercising
doing something important, like buying food
or going to the chemist, or for compassionate reasons.
When her eyes roamed the people in line, each 1.5 metres apart,
at chalked crosses on the pavement,
their faces as tight as their stretch Lycra,
she knew she was safe from the 'sitting police'.

I can't tell you – how isolated I feel.
She followed me to my car
saying, Be well. Be well,
as if she couldn't bear to leave me.

I can't say exactly when it was
that I heard the ambulance siren
pulling up next door. Or how it is now,
driving past her empty house,
feeling my feet anchored on a chalked cross,
as I wait to order,
the usual, because if I don't,
I'll go home totally bereft.

While Flattening the Curve

The whoosh of the first train
rattles the windows of the houses,

whines out of the tunnel destabilising foundations
so the people wide-awake beside the track

become the bullet train
whisked between regions

while the small bird with a sweet voice
peers down from the tree newly greened.

We need this quarantine, the self-isolation of the tracks,
fighting an invisible enemy. Perfect solo butterfly
swoops and flutters towards me.

As the small child who cannot play on the taped-up swing
sprints away from his dad who calls, 'How fast can you run?'

on a path through the park,
Mr Jenkins who lives alone

remembers his delivery at the back door.
No one will steal his fruit box, will not hover in the streets.

Bananas tucked into their skins,
sealed inside their own overripe brown flesh.

When the dog barks at seeing a tail-wagging puppy
running free on the grass,

he ponders, Tomorrow I'll slip my collar.
Then naps. The midday sun

glitters warmly on a driverless train
keeping its course, connecting the disparate pieces

as it's steered blindly, gripping the track
hurtling through the empty city.

The Road Back

The contours of despair slump
but the birds soar high

How we needed those birds when the ground
shifted beneath us with no rope to pull us back
and only birds with their superior aeronautical skills
knew how to swoop & dip & then rise again

The people kept their distance
clutching their satchels
of fear
I was just like them
the people spruiking ideas
plucked out of lucky dips then
batted across the pavements

But the birds so high in the air
existed in the moment
eyes wide open
the birds who had seen the planes
above the clouds
dirtying the skies
who noticed the change in the season
when we were not watching
what would they say to us
about taking our eyes off the bigger picture?

Waiting

The man who'd hoarded thousands of toilet rolls
is banned from selling them online
Now he's stuck with the stash he's hoarded
How many trips to the supermarket did he make?

The woman waiting
on the takeaway coffee queue
at the restaurant, We're trying to peer
through the fog, who knows when
we'll be able to travel again

The man who stands too close in the shopping
centre thinks it will be a long and rocky road back
If you saw him on the coffee queue and said,
please stand further away,
he may not respond well
not well at all

Steam rising from cappuccinos
Trudi calling out names from the line
before they bunch up too close
before the workmen still employed across the road
arrive with their circular saws & hammers & drills

Where is a way out of the year 2020?
Construction all day, particles expelled into the air
Trudi hopes the virus won't penetrate the coffee lids
thank goodness for the loyalty of locals
who keep her small business moving forward
in the right direction

Here

Each night the train
you cannot see
sounds a final journey
and the lightness which lifts you
in its healing promise all day
lets you down.

Now you pace,
heating up rooms,
pulling down blinds.

Into the silence
with its unknown destination,
conversations not yet had
or imagined.

Midnight threatens,
more enemy than
the worst enemy.

But you are here now
in this moment.

Do You Want To Try Me Out?

A man to a woman on a first date

White-headed gulls, which keep watch on a beach,
can live for forty-nine years.
Sleeping on the sea when it is calm,
they do not notice our presence.
Elongated legs,
a webbed, watery existence.
Still, a beak hooks
or a wing opens up
if we move.

What else but the flutter and flap of love?
Some say they've given up wishing & hoping & dreaming.
But those who find comfort in the stars
turn skywards for guidance.
If the sky could promise a soft landing,
the ground would welcome them.

Safe… The Pandemic

Everyone needs order,
clothes rehung,
cut roses secured in
a vase.

When we move,
when we place one foot
and then the other,
we can put small things in place,
an email to a friend in another country,
bags of rubbish carried out
to the bins.

Our brains, wired this way,
want the winter doona
smoothed squarely across the bed,
the freezer stocked, and remotes
in position.

After we get out, we have only to move
cautiously, surrounded by so much space.

Morning Storm

Weighted down…
pulled under
sucked in and again
surfacing for air
pulled in, dragged down
sucked into and under
disappearing into sand
unable to resist

the wind behind me
pushes…
me forwards

I reach the end of the island
turn around and return

my hair flies backwards
as I strain against the air

my shoes and socks
wait by the side of the cliff
I brush the sand off
one foot at a time
lace up my shoes
and walk up the hill

the pulsing of the waves
echoes in my ears
the rhythms of the ocean
the ebb and the flow
the uneven beat

The Bellydancer

She enters to the beat of a drum

from the top of the stairs
bare feet caress the steps
her young face veiled

silent anticipation
as she discards the layers
gyrating gently

until bared skin
in the middle
unlined and untamed

long blonde hair unleashed
against curves and crevices
folds of pink flesh

she ripples her back
half of her body
separating from the rest

shaking, shimmering, throbbing
her skirt flutters
hips held firm in gold

her eyes translucent
in the dream of her dance
enraptured

the breasts of a woman
the curve of belly
the spread of hips

arms reach out and up
like tendrils seeking –
soft armpits exposed

by the side of the room
his mouth stays open
as if frozen in surprise.

Change

I am like a butterfly
emerging from a dark cocoon
I squint into the sunlight.
Dare I open my eyes?

I struggle and I wriggle
because that's all I know.
I'm changing but I'm frightened
I know I have to grow.

My body once familiar
is forming great big wings.
I know they're there to help me
but I'm frightened to let go.

I long for my old comforts,
but they're no longer there.
The time to fly is coming,
and I must learn it soon.

As I prepare for lift off
I know I'm not ready yet.
The process is evolving
but first I must forget.

For now I am a butterfly
and this is how it is.
Very soon I'll learn to fly
and try out my new wings.

A butterfly can soar and leap
and travel through the air.
This is how I'd like to be
a creature light and fair.
To be up there above the ground
alive, awake, aware
that now I am a butterfly
and this is how it is.

End

There's my father
still clinging to life
determined as ever
grasping at the tubes.

A self-made man
for whom money
was a slippery commodity:
bankrupt twice; successful at the last.

Hard for him to love.
Given away as a boy,
he never found out
how to do it.

A wife offered little
from a separate room:
the door closed
in exhausted supremacy.

Success handed him security.
Cars and water views
dapper clothes and jaunty hats
books and classical music –

until muscular dystrophy.

In a country too-far-away
I see my father struggle.
What good am I?

This is what it feels like

When a single thought
may darken and trap,
terrify, for no apparent reason.
A storm
in your senseless head.
Whatever the thought,
think implosion of self
or crazy,
any thought you have held
in tenuous reality
like lead in the chest.
Say you were heavy-footed
downhill and it made you
want to stop. At midnight
driverless cars advance on you,
but where the hell is the brake?

Taking a Chance

This urban beach, its grassy slopes
worn away by the beaks of pigeons,
scavenging for cast-offs. Seagulls
with virgin feathers

offered me hope from endless nights.
I'd examined them carefully,
they communed in a different language.
'Enjoys walks on the beach,' everyone's profile said.

Today, the rush of traffic
accelerates through the air.
I'll apologise now for the noise,
a young man beside me says,

then mounts his bike.
A girl throws a leg over behind –
the roar shatters the blue.
Love needs courage –

the thing is, your eyes never left my face,
taking in every word.
You walked me back to my car.
kissed me gently on the cheek.

I opened the door –
resistance thrown to the wind.

My Friend Is Swiping & Scrolling

My friend in the dark hour before dawn. My friend with the ragged stomach who had a bad night. In a different hemisphere he is turning on the bedside light, rolling out of bed, pouring a cap of antacid at the kitchen bench. My friend who hasn't left his neighbourhood all year. My friend in London pining for how things used to be, for the Eurostar crossings to speak German and Spanish.

My friend scrolling through Facebook to see the faces of his family. My friend living alone who aches with aloneness. My friend the glass-half-full-kind-of-guy listening out for the early morning train thinking, we'll get through this, in time. My friend who sits through forty Zoom meetings every five days. A rush of nostalgic reflections but is everything nostalgia? We're all in this together.

The extroverted friend and the introverted one scrolling & swiping at home, the teenage friend whose father is hospitalised for a third time, my friend in China who sends me a red envelope, my friend in France dunking a croissant as she swipes left in greyish gloom, my friend in kurta pajamas beating a tabla drum, my friend in activewear driven to over-exercise, my friend who is addicted to social media like I am.

My friend in Israel   my stressed-out barista friend behind a coffee machine   my friend with only one kidney   my friend in palliative care under a sign I do not want visitors   my young friend who was warned at school about swiping & scrolling   my friend next door, who wonders if we are complaisant already   my friend who is feeling lethargic   my friend who hopes everyone will go back to work soon   my friend who tells me she has a problem wearing a mask   my friend who pretends not to see me on the street, even she must be on Zoom with others by now, so I let her go.

Scrolling will distract me from uncomfortable emotions as the cafes near me say takeaway only and the stores where I used to window-shop have empty frontages with To Lease signs and the famous writer I wish I'd had the courage to speak to when I had the chance, is diagnosed with dementia in another country, I snatch at memories of post cards sent back and forth. So who else should I pick up the phone and dial and say, Are you okay? Who else might I never see again?

All of us scrolling & swiping in the mornings and the afternoons and in the evenings near the hotel with the old TOOTH'S SHEAF STOUT Keeps you fit! poster telling us a tantalising beer with a dry finish and a medium body.

Distraction

My crimson bougainvillea
lives in a good-drainage pot.

I feed it fertiliser, and I keep
the soil a little on the dry side.

The bougainvillea thrives
with five hours of full sunlight a day,

scrambling vigorously up
a frame attached to the wall.

It flowers three times a year
with heavy pruning, lack of overwatering,

a fertiliser low in nitrogen and its roots
slightly restricted in a small container.

I watch the plant's flourishing from my bed:
its blooming brings beauty to my day.

It stops me from watching the latest news.

Hostilities

I worry about the ones
who disbelieve in science,
the ones on social media
with no qualifications
but a good command
of gobbledygook,
and the one who said
she'd had enough of wimps like me.

Scientists observe and calculate,
study the risks,
wave us across
as we wait by the side of the road,
even though the science of pandemics
is incomplete.

It takes a lot of guts sometimes
with those who are close to us.
Relatives, old school friends, intimates…
Anti-vaxxers still find arguments
to fire at us. I think of Aristotle's warning:
there is only one way
to avoid criticism –
do nothing, say nothing,
and be nothing.

Acknowledgements

Some of the poems in this collection were first published in the following journals and anthologies:

My Friend is Swiping & Scrolling, accepted for publication in *Quadrant*, 2022

Hostilities, *Quadrant*, June 2022

Survival, *Quadrant*, December 2021

White Ibis, *Quadrant*, December 2021

Someone I Don't Know Sideswiped My Car, *Quadrant*, April 2021

Distraction, *Burrow*, Old Water Rat Publishing, September 2021

Here, Blue Fringe Art & Literature Exhibition, 2021, Collected Works

Safe… The Pandemic, *Milestones*, Ginninderra Press, 2021

Quarantine, *Quadrant*, September 2020

His Coriander, *Quadrant*, September 2020

The Cellist, *Quadrant*, September 2020

Amber Puppy, *Mountain Secrets*, Ginninderra Press, 2019

Renewal, *Quadrant*, September 2019, and *Women's Ink!*, Winter 2021

Amber Puppy, *Quadrant*, September 2019

Taste, *Quadrant*, May 2019

Sixteen Is a Very Difficult Age, You Know, *Quadrant*, September 2018

Bronte Beach, *Wild*, Ginninderra Press, 2018

Between the Islands of the Pacific, *Quadrant*, June 2018

Elsewhere, *Quadrant*, December 2017

Lying On a Harbour Beach at Noon, *Quadrant*, January–February 2017

That's All You Can Do, *First Refuge: Poems on social justice*, Ginninderra Press, 2016

Her Amber Necklace, *The Thirteenth Floor*, XIV UTS Writers Anthology, 2000

Morning Storm, *Love the Word*, Poets Union Anthology, 1999

The Belly Dancer, *Untitled*, Poets Union Anthology, 1998

Change, *Free Range*, Poets Union Anthology, 1997

The Ladder and Its Dangers, longlisted for the 2019 joanne burns Microlit Award

In the Mall, selected as an entry in the Microflix Writers Awards 2019

About the Author

Libby Sommer is a regular contributor of stories and poems to *Quadrant* magazine. More than thirty of her short stories and thirty of her poems have been published in prestigious literary journals and anthologies. She has received grants from the Literature Board of the Australia Council and a Varuna Fellowship. She is the author of the novels *My Year With Sammy* (2015), *The Crystal Ballroom* (2017), *The Usual Story* (2018), *Stories From Bondi* (2019) and *Lost In Cooper Park* (2020). Her debut novel, *My Year With Sammy*, was Pick of the Week, *Sydney Morning Herald*, and winner of the Society of Women Writers Fiction Book Award 2016. *My Year With Sammy* was also shortlisted in Seizure's Viva La Novella Competition 2015 and the UK's Mslexia Competition 2014. Her most recent novel, *Lost in Cooper Park*, was a notable entry in Seizure's Viva La Novella Competition 2018 and the European Disquiet International Literary Book Contest.

Libby Sommer lives in Sydney, Australia.
She blogs at https://libbysommer.wordpress.com/
Her website is http://libby.sommer.net.au/

www.ingramcontent.com/pod-product-compliance
Lightning Source LLC
Chambersburg PA
CBHW070336120526
44590CB00017B/2910